THAT NIGHT WE WERE RAVENOUS

BOOKS BY JOHN STEFFLER

POETRY

An Explanation of Yellow (1980)
The Grey Islands (1985)
The Wreckage of Play (1988)
That Night We Were Ravenous (1998)
Helix: New and Selected Poems (2002)

FICTION

The Afterlife of George Cartwright (1992)

FOR CHILDREN

Flights of Magic (illustrated by Shawn O'Hagan) (1987)

THAT NIGHT
WE WERE
RAVENOUS

JOHN STEFFLER

McCLELLAND & STEWART

Library and Archives Canada Cataloguing in Publication

Steffler, John, 1947–
That night we were ravenous : poems / John Steffler.

Originally published: 1998.
ISBN 978-0-7710-8266-5

I. Title.

PS8587.T346T47 2007   c811.'54   C2007-903666-X

We acknowledge the financial support of the Government of Canada
through the Book Publishing Industry Development Program and that
of the Government of Ontario through the Ontario Media
Development Corporation's Ontario Book Initiative. We further
acknowledge the support of the Canada Council for the Arts and the
Ontario Arts Council for our publishing program.

Typeset in Minion by M&S, Toronto
Printed and bound in Canada

ANCIENT FOREST
FRIENDLY

McClelland & Stewart Ltd.
75 Sherbourne Street
Toronto, Ontario
M5A 2P9
www.mcclelland.com

1 2 3 4 5   11 10 09 08 07

I dedicate these poems with love to Al Pittman, Marilee Pittman, Ken Livingstone, Randy Maggs, Linda Williams, Anne Pinsent, Gail Brownlee, Paul, Harold, and Dorothy Steffler, Edith and Alban. There are drinks in the kitchen, please help yourselves.

The section "Borrowed Home" is for Jane Rabnett, Ralph and Eve Bates, Klaus and Marlene Pfeiffer, and David Chater.

ACKNOWLEDGEMENTS

My thanks to the editors of the following journals in which some of the poems in this collection first appeared: *Poetry Canada Review*, *TickleAce*, *Event*, *Canadian Literature*, *Slow Dancer*, *The Malahat Review*, *The Fiddlehead*, and *The New Quarterly*.

Excerpts on pp. 16-17 are from *Traveller's Guide to the Geology of Newfoundland and Labrador*, by Stephen Colman-Sadd and Susan Scott, Government of Newfoundland and Labrador, Department of Mines and Energy, and Natural Resources Canada. 1994. Reprinted with permission.

For support at various times I am grateful to the Canada Council, to the Newfoundland and Labrador Arts Council, and to Sir Wilfred Grenfell College, Memorial University.

I wish to thank Jane Rabnett, David Chater, Marlene and Klaus Pfeiffer, and Ralph and Eve Bates for their kind hospitality.

For their editorial assistance I am grateful to Ellen Seligman and Peter Buck. I am especially indebted to Don McKay for helping to select and edit the poems in this collection. Talking with Don about the habits and movements of words is a very special pleasure.

CONTENTS

BORROWED HOME

ANIMAL

IN A MAKESHIFT BLIND

START OF A TRAIL

a flattened bird's nest

cleft moose print

clusters of rose-purple
cones in the black spruce boughs
gum-beaded
dusted
with their own yellowish dust

good tender ache of things
needing to open

Above Cabot Strait, the props
of the Dash-8 shake and grumble,
screwing us deeper
into the pure Newfoundland
cloud, north, farther
north where I live, the whole
cabin jiggling
loudly, the children
straining their feverish
voices – and it already feels
like home, the few people
aboard talking in groups
in the aisle, ordering
one another drinks – and I
wouldn't change where I'm going,
into my awkwardness, my broken
marriage, troubles richer
than Voisey's Bay, my
unexpected life off
all the maps I'd ever imagined,
the unfamiliar heart
of where we all live.

darkly faceted,
eager,
yakking and glancing around at the jewellery-shop shelves,
then, lifting arms that darken the air,
sweeps everything to its chest.

It opens its mouth
and clearly wants food.

The sea gangs in gay and pointy,
weed green;
the smell of it gives you hungry lungs;
its thud feels good as fucking;

then it drags the stones of the beach back, rattling them,
all the bones people have left, skulls
empty of pleasures,
ownerless teeth.

The sea gangs in
buttered with morning light, throwing its lace hem at your
    bachelor's boots,
and you snap photos, kneeling,
panting,
pen poems,

and the waves, as they draw themselves up to dive,
for a second,
go thin and glassy,

give glimpses into a place where pale shapes tilt and
    stretch
like long green boxes
in a stone cell.

CEDAR COVE

If your wharf is washed away
it will come to Cedar Cove –
Wild Cove on the maps or
Capelin Cove. If your boat

goes down it will sail to Cedar
Cove piece by piece.
And your uncle, should he not come back
from his walk on Cape St. George,

will be found grinning among
the glitter of barkless roots
laths struts stays
stringers and frayed rope

in Cedar Cove, where no
cedars have ever grown,
but that's what the local people
call it. The water horizon

topples straight down
on Cedar Cove over
and over, box cars
falling, loads of TNT.

And the wind will not let you speak
in Cedar Cove, which could
be called Deaf Cove
or Lobotomy Cove, will not

let you think or stand straight;
the shrunk trees writhe
and have the wrong kinds
of leaves, but their roots spread

wide in Cedar Cove,
whose gravel is soft compared
to its air. We have come to Cedar
Cove overland, my love

and I, having been lost
at sea in another way.
All day we scatter
ourselves through the noise

and whiteness, learning the thousand
ways things can be taken
apart and reassigned –
the boot sole impaled on the shattered

trunk, the rust flakes,
the bone flakes encrusting a bracelet
of kelp – losing our pictures
of home, stick by stick.

After Cedar Cove,
what will be left of us?

HARRY'S HARBOUR

for the first time it seems
comfort and cold go together

coming down off the rock
hill in the lustre of ending rain
the road swings near the barred
harbour,
              wharfs and thick-painted hulls,
birch only coming into leaf
the twentieth of June
                    green
frill on earth's old ruptures, heavings, high
islands, shadowed coves

I see wheel tracks on the beach rock bar
past the last homes,
                stacks
of winter-cut logs along its side,
and head there to camp

out of the truck our senses go
like dogs into the fenceless
space,
         sea wind smelling of ice, cut spruce

rocks clang underfoot like broken tiles

good at disguise,
my thoughts refuse to be thoughts, cross
the dark harbour

        bob among boats

LONG POINT

cosmographer's dream of perspective

past Lourdes, past
Black Duck Brook the peninsula's
limestone spine tapers for fifteen miles northeast
into the Gulf of St. Lawrence

road into whitecaps and air

shedding its margins

road to the loss of road   out
of solidity

I walk that windy spit to its vanishing point
where opposing surfs merge
where Port au Port Bay and its sky and its weather
lose to the open gulf
and the slick whittled rock I stand on plunges
a titanic eel

for a long time I lean letting my face ride like a kite
on the turbulence

wave noise twists
to a throat I could slip through in a dive

part of me does dive,
I feel tracings, shadows go with the strong pull
out of my skin

into another place
where I must be walking even now

SEA COAST NEAR PARSON'S POND

Too many stones:
the speckled egg
the sleeping face
the ones with fine white moon canals
one with script

the silky hip emerging from the sand .

those with boils
the vulva stones both pinched and eager, giant seeds

I stop at the good ones, picturing them on the patio by the
    potted lobelia
then stride ahead renouncing the storehouse of home

where they dull and go blank

The sea's smell is a hunger for distance

How can I bring back what I love as a cure for my
    helplessness?

The land loosens here
The continent's history swims
slowly out of itself

This blind love of the future
is what I want
grafted into my heart

into the lake under my tongue

BLURRED WREATH

Nearing the timberline,
the woodcutters' wet track enters a lap
in the mountain's body, pocket
of heat where I stop to eat lunch:

snow and peridotite scree high through a keyhole
of spruce, the place where I'm heading, pure
heartbeat.

On a stump
in a bay of May sun, I sit among knots
of new leaves. Curled ferns in their white fuzz
cauls are being born, clumped, blindly
lifting brown crust.

I talk to a puddle
of black peat, perfect slurry of marrow and earth's
juice. Reflective dents on its surface are pools
in the old tracks of moose – clear
trickle at one moss lip – its roots
deep in the mountain's body. Some

king lies chuckling there,
some god in the shape of a blurred
wreath or coiled shell is speaking in thin
green lines that flame in the air,

green lust vessels with fine
points brooming, trembling, reaching
out

AT WOODY POINT

the sun comes up where
the moon did   only hours ago
across South Arm over the mountain wall –

    diagonal half moon
    jutting
    unexpected and late,
    shark's fin in a school of stars,
      high autumn stars,
    cold smell of the woods above
    when I stepped out to piss,
      the lawn crisp,
    dew that was almost frost –

and this morning the shadows of branches
white on the grass

and the stove creaks and mutters
coming awake   the room occupied
by the bitten shadows of leaves, blurred,
tripled minnows of light,   music

that takes you into its unexpected
depths,

surprises you
with how you can swim

TRAVELLER'S GUIDE TO THE GEOLOGY OF NEWFOUNDLAND AND LABRADOR

with thanks to Stephen Colman-Sadd and Susan Scott

Drive to Moreton's Harbour, and take the road
that circles the east side of the harbour
warm air through the open windows, I drive
with a hand half under your loose shorts, your

leg a warm vein of gold *turn left onto a*
gravel road that continues around the harbour,
and park where a picket fence encloses two
satellite dishes hair loose on your cheek,

your eyes fix on the unfolding bay, then you
read again *walk along the path between*
the fence and the high rocky hill; it crosses
the neck to some old fenced fields from the back

of the seat my fingers fall into your hair,
discover your spine's soft nuggets *as you enter*
Little Harbour, note the rough flow texture
of the lava on your right (my heart's needle

leaping) *and the smooth glacially polished*
and fluted diabase outcrops on your left
we carry our lunch over the old convulsions,
crackling lichen, crabs' claws dropped

by gulls *beyond the fields on the shore,*
and best seen at low tide, are pillows,

and splattered volcanic ash and lava fragments
wind flutters the pages, flutters your blue

top, my hand sails lightly in that sea
the beds have been folded so they are nearly
vertical and compression has formed a cleavage
almost at right angles to the bedding I kneel

smelling the basalt, the rhyolite hot
in the sun, the pegmatite dikes, smell
of old burning *small holes in some of the*
rocks were once gas bubbles in the molten

lava I spread the blanket, carefully
place the oranges, the plums on the jagged
stones *these features indicate an explosive*
volcanic environment you close the book.

We both look at the sea

On Little Bay Islands, after taking a nap in a gravel pit in the back of the truck in baking heat, the windows most of the way up to keep out blackflies, we shook our flushed faces and started up the dusty road toward Ken's Lounge, hoping to get some supper and a beer, having failed to find an open store or restaurant or even a functioning pop machine all that Sunday afternoon,

and fell in behind a truck loaded with gravel slowly climbing the hill in a fog of dust, finally passed it on a down-grade curve, waving to the bearded driver, and pulled into Ken's parking lot, but the place was locked up, so got back on the road to town, in the gravel truck's wake again, and eventually passed him again, waving again,

then sat on the town wharf, boatless, strewn with engine parts, the encircling town doubled head-down in the mahogany evening water, and watched the one spot of activity at the crab plant across the harbour, the gravel truck backing up to a dip in the loading yard and dumping his loud dust, then we crossed the island's hills again to the ferry dock and backed on just ahead of the empty truck, waving to the bearded driver and his pretty daughter, who we now notice beside him in the cab, both of them grinning, waving back,

and after passing small black islands and one vast whale-shaped iceberg, smooth as a moon, burning, compacted white, after watching the light on the mercury sea, the whole world gone to grey silk and toffee, forgetting our hunger the while, we landed and headed through

Coffee Cove and Little Bay to Beachside, hoping to find a secluded place to park for the night,

and found an open variety store where we bought jam-jams and Pepsi for supper and told the expressionless woman behind the counter about our trip to Little Bay Islands, and she said her husband had been there that day delivering a load of gravel,

so we walked out thinking about that, and then drove through Beachside, where the only activity, far down the road, was a large man riding an unruly pony, tilting backwards, sideways, barely hanging on, while beside him a girl fought with another pony on a lead,

and as we drew near, following their slow procession in first gear, their veering from side to side, we recognized the bearded truck driver, now wild and Irish in flapping coat, his tall daughter scampering bare-legged, swatting a flank, her tangled gold hair flying.

They waved – dark bright smiles, like palmfuls of bullets – we waved, crawling behind them, entranced by those twelve possessed legs.

we wake up warm under quilts
in the back of the truck

night rain has passed and the flame-furred sun
huge and clearly a creature
is perched on the headland in cloudless blue

peninsula blue, cold
unusable

the cove at the foot of the beach rock bar spreads
to the earth's edge

night had been near to freezing
I wipe the breath-fogged windows for the view
for the sun's warmth
we drink from the cold whisky bottle
to clean our mouths, roll
together
the sea is fucking you, you say, rocking
on top of me to the slosh of waves

the truck door open, sun
on our faces, wind somehow
not coming in, black
gleams on the water close to us, curved

motion of whales' backs stitching liquid
and light, a long slow
seam,
loud puff of their swimmer's breaths

both of us thinking here's where I want to stay,
would a house be for sale?
would we ever fit in? would we
break some spell?

wash with aching water naked on the stones
circle the place on the map

drive on

SINCE EARLY MAY

have been using the camera to come at what's
here: spring's first
devices: sticks

poking folded green fans out of their tips,
green knobs of marsh marigolds getting
hot yellow, flinging their centres out

a danger to look at without smoked glass

I go through the photos bringing
the fervour indoors, float

my heart again on its current

its pressure under my throat

ferns uncurling words

IN THE FIRST WEEK OF JUNE

Southern emotion moved up in the night,
and we woke to green steady rain,
pasture smell,
our house a dovecote of shadows – winter's
thin diagrams had fled from the walls –
and we stayed undressed, taking our coffee from room
    to room,
opening windows, listening,
sheltering inside an instrument played by a god,
the shingles incredibly good in the long riffs,
pittered ditties and grave claims,

the gurgle,

jokes in the gravel under the eaves –

I stand in the back door
in something sweeter than sleep,
the glassy porch boards pocked and dancing,
the naked bride poplars trying on green
earrings, pearls

The Arbol del Tule
first sprouted when Christ was born,
according to a man from Oaxaca,
and is now the world's biggest tree – bright
crowds at its fenced bole snapping photos,
shrill nimbus of birds in its craggy crown,
the tree! the tree! the tree!

Now,
back from palms, plantains, cactus, mangoes, necking
couples angled everywhere on the ground under jacarandas,
oleanders, hearts and initials carved in the cool
tentacles of agaves,

again
I'm walking
on the crusted rocks of the Newfoundland Blomidons,
browns and greys,
rocks meant to be under the sea,
backsided landscape,
mirror-back, moon-back, mask-back, bootsole, gaps
between words spliced together, mystery
I almost think I have figured out

I go at it again
on my knees with a camera,
my face for an hour over a puddle of black bog:
arbol, *arbol*, young ferns
surfacing here

same sacred vein

The morning is dark and a wet fall wind
is tossing the thinning boughs,
the bottom edge of the window fogged with fine beads.

I abandon the corporation of myself.
I do not sit down at my desk at nine o'clock,
I do not dig into the pile of unfinished poems
or write to writers and editors.

When the frilled skirts and speeches are put away,
where do the actors go,
the lovers, when they part?
I will follow them into their dim rooms, wait

in the hours buzzing with silence, the sound
of breathing and creaking wood.
In the backyard, the bed I had started to dig

is dark and sodden,
stones lie scattered on the lawn. Beyond
the Eastern Lakes,
in hills few people visit, autumn

walks with the same rough grace.
Inclusive animal.
There are gods whose origins need to be questioned.

Do they ask you to pose in a daily
coffin?
Man-made gods always
want us to kill ourselves.

This morning I lie in a makeshift blind and watch
what the animal does.
He wanders around in crowds of air. I cannot

distinguish him from the worn leaves rubbing,
the yellows.
The smell of the earth is the same
as his skin.

STILL LOOSE AND CIRCLING YOU

FOR MY EXECUTION

For my execution,
the spot I choose is just to the south
of where the barn used to stand, a zone
where the grass rippled and posed like a handsome animal,
sleek on a century of barnyard loam,

where our horse, Pat, lay down one Saturday morning
and I sat on his flank grinning and squinting into the
east to have my picture taken
and he didn't care,

my sister, housecoated, holding the camera, her neck
and shoulders bitten away by the sun, the milk-house
beside her with its unused well under
a clutter of planks,
the fieldstone throat I would peer down, into
the past, watching a pebble fall – once in a drought,
to water the garden, my father pumped out its
stench, its corpses, liquid blots of fur –

a spot I wanted only to leave,
the cedar rail paddock we built in a bad
mood, the tramped grass steamy as seaweed in the migraine
of noon, lending myself like a slave as we
dug the holes,
postponing my ownership,
reserving my willingness
for my own life, somewhere over the rim of that ploughed
green bowl.

I will kneel and wait for it,
facing east.

THE COBS FATTEN, BUT EVERY SO OFTEN

Mountains come back to these soft lands,
these dairies. Still after millions of years
their ghosts march through the sky at first light
seizing the last of the darkness in crags
and chasms, rolling grey
foothills over the sun.

Earth trembles again, black
cracks split the air – overhead the outline of horned
crowns, flint weapons, immense shoulders clad in skins
of bears – rough mockery rumbles down,
the old power to ravage and burn.

Heat,
earth's excitement vining, swirls
I perch in like a toucan, lonely impatient
toucan –
            light from a hundred green
acres spills over my writing hand, the card
stuck to my wrist, skin
beaded with sweat, powdered with small
seeds –
            "Sequined and green, I'm
beckoning you aboard this house the birds
and raccoons share with me – racket
of bugs – even the loam's on a slow
boil rolling with moles – everything
voting yes with its body, making
more of itself"
                – picture your gasp
as you step from the airport door –
back-float on heat –
                        "Sunscreen
is all the clothing you'll need," I scrawl
for the fifth time in as many days –
                                    wet
the stamp on my chest, standing squinting
down the bare lane

Crickets can't stand it in Newfoundland,
so you need a good house there to keep
the silence out, the buzz of "folly! folly!"
your ears make in an empty space.

Here on the grand banks of southern
Ontario, schools of birds plunge in the blue
air and crickets build walls of sound more
full of curly depths than William Morris wallpaper,
than the paintings of Henri Rousseau.

You can sit naked here in any
windowless old shack and ply your trade quite happily,
whatever it might be. You've got
support. So many other creatures choose to live here too
and love it.
Just listen to them carry on.

But in Newfoundland, the houseless man is
naked all the way to the stars, to the troll-noggined sea,
scowling over the rock in its famous enmity.

Build your walls thick there and
stay indoors, filling the lighted air
with the music of men.

EDGE OF A FIELD

squirts and burbles of birdsong
I wear for a hat

a woodpecker ten feet above me
is what I now know best

striking the word *wood*
in every language on earth

*   *   *

some fellow hidden in the grass is showing
off
eating a stalk of celery with large
false teeth

GREEN GIVING

This green shower caught in the arms
of the wind, green memory of rain
after the rain has passed: young

elm leaves fountaining down slight
boughs, green fingerprints, like
notes sprayed out of the grand

piano by Debussy's hands, gracing
my window, armfuls cast from above,
green giving: sparrows plunge

in, deft brown strokes of the feathered
brush, finding the shadows that wait
for them like cool suits of clothes.

EATING OUTDOORS

We tossed our oranges up
and caught them
                    got into a rhythm,
tossed them over and over out of sight
in the June sun.

An orange becomes something else
when you do that, pouch of juice, yo-yo sun
coming down in your hands.

Looking up running barefoot seeing only
orange and sky, I was never so
drunk again until six years later at the end
of grade ten, trees

carouselled, finally I ran face
first into the same
grass my feet were feeling, my body had
stretched right around the planet or a huge
green belly had come around some corner
I hadn't seen.

THE BREEZE ITSELF

The breeze itself
breathes in and out,
finding form in the trees and grass
with a sound of releasing, a sliding
rush into dreams, into the past,
which is where the wind always lives,
outside our bedroom windows where
we were young, where it still resides,
                                        circling,
swooping down with its arms made only
of what arms feel, shivers of holding, love,
touch of whatever kind, filling and
fading, the way everything will,
teaching us this,
the shape of history and hills, dresses and hair,
gladness – how it occupies the rooms
we open for it,
patience – how we keep those empty places
in repair.

the sound of rain
at dawn at the open window, falling
from wooden eaves among lilacs, clicking
and pattering pebbles and puddled earth, the air

thick with assurance (a mother hushing her
child to sleep, applause of countless small
hands over the growing wheat), and the breeze lifts,
the sweet history of earth pours in, turning
the curtain aside in a gust of your own childhood,
still loose and circling you,
damp spirits of earth, youngest of things

(moss roof, stone walls, the lane compounded of charcoal
and dung, the barrels, the orchards, tall weeds darkened
with rain, and the rooster under a gable restraining its
cry; we rise late, glad of the wood for a fire to take off
the chill; most human morning, air most shaped like human
skin, our arms touching, our children half asleep on our
laps at the table, on chairs at the open window, the bead
curtain of rain)

and the breeze shifts and the rain
shifts key the way leaves turn from green to white
in a sudden wind, as a wave slides over sand, stirring
the writing there, as a wave of sleep slides
through your day's first thoughts,
blurring them, a curtain of soft rain
falling over your thoughts, your
thoughts falling, you
falling back into sleep

FEBRUARY FIRST

beyond the glass doors: light
that hurts,
snow marked by a few bird tracks, scant
purple cuneiform

near the house wall little flakes
of ice, weightless
sparks
are flitting around in the breeze
like static on a video screen, as though
excessive light
condensed in crystals.

I want to respond
somehow, drink tea straight
from the pot, jump through the glass
and hang like Nureyev
all day,
the burst glass chiming around me
pure outer space

DARK ROOM

I have burned so little
of my fuel
have not burned my sister, set her
scream free

have not burned my father's
anger

not wanting to add to the damage I act
as though I have no country
only a job, a house,
a night to go shopping

furniture in the shapes of animals
is still there in the room
though the lights are out

the dog-headed chairs
the trunks stuffed with human
skins I could hold up like clothes
and recognize

Sitting outside with a book
for the first time this year –

                      on the blue walls
the birds are scribbling
wildly with brilliant
crayons,
        and the spirals and saws and mazes
tangle and fade
and are overlaid with more bird iconography,

more landscape according to Blue Jay, Grackle, Starling,
Robin.

I want to paint the inside walls of my skull with these
     scrawls
which are more useful than all the buildings of Waterloo,
all the blunders of roads and suburbs.

The blue is a tongue on which all dissolves,
is swallowed
            with a kind of smile – space and time being
actually pleasure, narrative
unafraid of an end.

Two grackles greasy with cobalt, viridian, shoulder
their way through the branches, taste
each frost-baked apple left on the tree.

                          Small,
small in the blue, a pale

hawk circles on heavy wings, thinking of fruit
of another kind.

Grave consciousness
that encloses consciousness. Today

there's no point thinking of him.

Near noon it will happen.
For twenty-seven years there will not be another;
and will we be alive then, will we be together?
As the birds grow anxious in the trees and the light
    tightens to smoked blue,
the sad thought of you alone in your studio, me alone
    here with my gadgets of words
is a darkening that will not be put right.
And I walk as fast as I can through the bled streets,
    but your studio's empty.
And will the dark come then while I'm in a parking lot,
    mistaken,
unconnected to this place or that?
I put myself into your absent body,
into your feelings and face, your own restless loneliness,
and I head toward the post office, the store, thinking
    somehow this is a test of my intuition,
of our sympathies,
telepathy or delusion,
apart or together when the snapshot from heaven is taken,
    this memory happening now,
this crucial memory,
and there you are coming toward me carrying milk,
your face sad and tilted toward the ground
    until you see me –
the clap of gladness we make coming together, lined up
    with the sun and moon at our heads,
the earth at our feet,

the blurred shadows of branches trembling around us,
    about to come undone, about to break
into script or tears or racing
flame.

So hard to parcel an event
without lying. A flood running *out*
in every direction, including up and down, an
ignition, a flowering, a turning inside out, an animal
busy in the wild, and you decide tick
tack toe connect the dots across this thing,
and that represents it all?
We can extrapolate the rest?
It's true,
old boxes, old jars
hum with a kind of diffused meaning, old
medieval coffers, Tang bowls hold so much more
than wine or thimbles or emptiness. Words
too are like that,
the old standard containers you crack your mind
into like an egg. Even choosing
a chain of events is an equally old language,
even saying "I" and "it"
and "happened," the old customs are there.
But it wasn't *like* that,
there was no climax and denouement,
or there *was*, but the denouement was a climax too
and the story went on in another direction, which
my ghost, watching from under the water inside my heart,
found more interesting, more
significant.
With the eclipse coming on and me running to find
Shawn to be together at the astronomical tourist attraction,
the cosmic wedding photograph,
it suddenly hit me
that I was leaving my daughter at home,

that she had told me that morning she'd dreamt
of the eclipse – that she'd burnt her eyes looking at it –
and we had talked about how, when she was very young,
she had worried that our cat would be blinded in the back
yard during an eclipse in Pasadena, Newfoundland,
and it hit me that maybe she wanted me to be with her again
poking a hole in a playing card to catch the black sun
on an envelope,
and I was abandoning her,
so when I found Shawn, we turned
and walked quickly home, me carrying the milk, past
a mother duck minding fifteen newly hatched ducklings,
past woods full of trilliums as rich a white
as Diego Rivera's lilies, under the coral
buds on the maples, among the spooky
blurred shadows, home,
where we acted as if nothing strange was going on,
where we washed dishes and I made a pinhole in cardboard
that didn't work
and we talked about what movies were coming,
about playing pool, about getting
into university.

BRICKS, FACES, WORDS

In Kitchener (Berlin in my great-grandmother's
letters: "p. s. I have a boarder lies in bed till
half past eight it is a lady") they are knocking
the best buildings down, the distilleries, felt
factories, shoe factories, the Victorian brick
walls discomposed, falling mosaics of faces,
group portraits, people so naturally quick
to make a community is what always worked
in the owner's favour, good morning Frieda I see
you forgot your umbrella too my hair is soaked
I just saw Otto Leuning with a daisy in his jacket
pocket – the whistle, the pulleys jolt and turn,
the slack belts wind to their steady taut
howl, the cutters, the stitchers, riveters,
skivers clank, startled with power, the workers
enter their patterned movements, the chopped-off
sentences to be finished at lunch or at 4 o'clock

speech used to overlook, to be stronger than any
disaster, any machine yanking the body, any
diphtheria tetanus typhoid stroke, smells
and sorrows, secrets – words stitched into prayers,
chip-carved with long pointed diamonds, painted
with gardens and trotting mares, words that forbade
words, paved the crazy heart under, gave
the nightmare no means of transmission, the naked
feet solid floor at the bedside, good morning oh
the stove is smoking, is the wind from the east?

I undo the generations of strength, fix words
to minutes, to process (why would I want to?)

drown in the long-diked sea of dreams, speak
of the labour and anger under the Sunday picnics,
weddings, funerals, family photos on the lawn.

I live with them now that they've lost their
bodies, with their ungathered unpresented
selves, I walk Weber, Breithaupt, Ahrens,
Queen, their hidden hearts in the air, Brauns,
Millers, Leunings, Hoelschers, Stefflers,
the fallen yellow bricks holding their soft
German voices: look at what people throw away.

In Waterloo
the people keep their bodies clean. They work
at avoiding disease and sign
contracts to have their lawns kept green.

On the long drive from work they think about
Helen in marketing,
Theseus in systems analysis.
They negotiate the landscape of their jobs
like Sherpas in a dream,

and their cars slide into their garages and the garage doors
close electronically and the people ascend into the
great code of the Canadian Tire catalogue, into the
Bible of Sears Canada Inc.

Time does not course through the people of Waterloo and
their possessions the way it courses through other matter in
the natural world,
no dissolved Ojibwa or Iroquois lie in the earth under their
homes,
no large trees ever roared and thrashed in their
neighbourhood,
no mastodons sniffed one another's arses there, no glaciers
lurk in the memory of the land, what land could I be
thinking of? there is no land,
no pioneer ever walked behind a horsedrawn plough,
no one was ever born there, nobody holds a picture
of a previous state of the place in their mind,
nobody ever *saw* it, certainly nobody ever died looking
at it or remembering it.

48

The houses of Waterloo float in a void.

They bulge out of the TV screen like bubbles bulging
out of a wire loop
and break free, wobbly,
shimmering.

They are television screen hernias,
the houses of Waterloo,

bubbles blown out of L.A.,
hovering, wobbling –

oh, the people inside them *look so young*!

NEAR THE CONFLUENCE OF
THE CONESTOGA AND THE GRAND

the road drops into the valley,
mud-stubble corn lots,
fine green flats once brimming from bluff to bluff
    with glacial melt – the old giant world with mammoths
    and ice mountains straggling north – legend
    of that strength still in the air, grey April sky
    tumbling over,
the Grand now a runnel in this wide track, brown
scuttle,
dirt from the ploughing, the ditches and towns,
Chevy River,
Uniroyal, CIL – it doesn't know these names,
still filling its valley invisibly, unconcerned with
    the size of its flow, what stuff it carries.

When we are gone it will rise and clear itself
quickly,
busy with sturgeon and char.

On a bank matted with flood chaff I stand,
saying *my queen, my queen,*
my goddess –
the woman I love, starving, chained to the cellar
floor – *have I hurt you in some unconscious*
fit?

On his seventy-eighth birthday my father stands with the screen door slightly open, softly whistling, tossing peanuts to blue jays. "Look at the young ones," he says. "They're as big as their parents but still want to be fed."

Among the things on my desk the painting of Hamlet on the Stratford program keeps tripping my thoughts. His hungry unwell head. A flesh of worry the only difference between himself and the crowned skull he's staring at. His right hand's fingers curl at his chin exactly the way I pick at my beard. Spooky mirror. I get rid of the thing.

Dedication to something beyond yourself. As for example the weeds in the ravine behind the lawns off Craigleith Avenue. Tall grasses, milkweed in flower, hawthorn trees. The long young gorgeous body, buried, sectioned, here and there showing through.

The young jays are confused. They watch their parents pick the peanuts up, and copy them, then drop the peanuts, hunch their wings helplessly, open their red mouths and go cheep. But get no attention. Look around flustered, try feeding themselves again.

Last night I dreamt an insane dream. How do you tell an insane dream from a sane one? It does not smell as though it belongs to you. It burns artificial fuel. It has no mythology.

One young jay gets as far as holding a peanut between its toes on the edge of the porch, draws its head back to peck, then loses its balance and falls out of sight. My father wheezes with pleasure. These clownish imperatives. To have young, to squabble, to hoard, to try and get free. Poor simple god.

White-faced, he used to clap on his hat and go into the cellar to work with his tools. Wanted out of his own clamorous script, the love plots, the tears and appeals. Now he whistles and throws food and watches it all mimed back, miniature, innocent.

LITTLE WREN

My mother would kind of like to tell about
the spouse-swapping going on in their small
town, "Three families – two teachers and the
school secretary – they all just . . ." but
my father looks sullen and wonders if that
little wren he sees out through
the window will stay around.

"Will they come to a feeder?" my mother asks.

"No," he says, exhausted and desolate,
"they only eat bugs."

I had dropped some papers in a crowded subway train – or was it a party? – and a man in a business suit picked them up and kept them, with a mocking look, so I felt in my pocket for the knife that I got twenty-five years ago in Utrecht, that I thought I'd lost the time I went off and started a novel, that the police confiscated in the airport in Mexico City and a stewardess handed back in a brown envelope after we'd touched down in Toronto in driving snow. And I clicked it open and, holding it like a carving tool, my hand along the back of its blade, I touched the tip to a pulsing vein in the man's neck, and he held out my fallen papers, dropped them into my bag.

What papers were they? I can't tell you that, but I'd been collecting them and they meant a great deal to me, and I hurried away thinking I won't do that again with my feeble penknife. What if he'd had a gun? What if he hadn't trusted me?

I slowed the car I was driving to a stop in the country darkness, at the end of the lane in the loose smell of fields. The old house was still there in its own time and place, not replaced by factories. Its living-room windows lit, partly hidden by the dark shapes of lilacs and spruce.

I was like a bird gliding in to land who thinks it is landscape, who has no concept of *bird*, and everything happened fast then. I left the car on the grass just past the point in the lane where it turns sharply south toward the house, the place where strangers from the city would sometimes park thinking they weren't quite on our land yet, or thinking we were the same as city people, deaf and oblivious, that we wouldn't notice them there. But we were as keen as spiders, we'd heard the gravel popping under their tires a quarter-mile away. And the strange men would maybe follow the grass-covered track to the west and look at our garden, take a tomato or two or some cobs of corn or poke through the fallen barns for antiques, while I watched from the kitchen window fingering the twenty-two.

I was out in the country dark, in the fields' loose smell, running as hard as I could to the house. Someone was in it. A woman I saw through the window, a stranger in brown clothes with long hair. I didn't want her to see me, I didn't linger to spy, I flew from the northeast side to the south and in through the back kitchen door, in past the cookstove into the kitchen, noises were coming out of me to tell her I'd found her I was back I was huge, I was beyond words beyond any kind of face beyond a body, I was only using it crudely, and I rushed on her as she turned, a brown blur, a woman, possibly frightened, possibly more solid than me.

WILD PEAR

In the car coming home
from church, my father
was angry, and my mother
cried without touching
her face. She set
the table and sat
and the tears fell
on her dress. He pushed
his chair back then
and left, and I watched
from the window over
the sink as he went
west past the barns.

Surprised at myself,
I stepped into sunlight
and followed him,
kept him in sight
in the back lane
between fields of oats,

but then he was gone,

and I walked on
gazing, gazing,
and gave up
beside a bank of
raspberries, shadows
and glitter, and there

suddenly saw him,
motionless among leaves,
smiling at me
with a face inside
his face, embarrassed
and knowing and caught,
lying deep in the grass
under a wild pear tree –
half in a fox hole
was what I thought –
and young-looking,

my father as much
of a boy as me.

Over the hills to the south on the edge of the city the bombs had begun to go off. My parents said nothing about it, but their faces stiffened and all our routines were subtly adjusted to getting away when the time finally came. This was in the early 1960s. The effect of the bombs was strange. The explosion clouds stood in the sky as though solid and only gradually changed, suggesting the configuration of tall buildings. The shock waves came in a bedlam of heavy machinery, and when the clouds at last dissolved, the buildings were there on the crest of the hill, thousands of windows catching the red sun, and the yellow earth movers snorting, prowling, edging our way. More clouds and blasts. Closer. Bombs that dropped office desk factories, signs saying Riviera Drive, Sandalwood Crescent, bodies in cars dashing for hamburgers at noon, desert of glittering shingle roofs where there had been trees. My sister had gone at night into the uproar. My parents argued, everything needed packing or leaving. I put some clothes in a canvas bag and left one hot morning at dawn, dust quickly hiding the old white house, the trees, and made my way here where I can't stay long.

BORROWED HOME

AT THE PIGI CAFE, ANO POTAMIA

Next to the famous spring flashing
naked out of her stonework portico, the cafe men
are gabbing over a truck, the hood up,
the waiter lighting his nimble
cigarette, the brook

of their syllables tumbling
down through the garden tables.

Having walked through noon in the crackling
hills, I stop at their side
for refreshment,
glad not to know what they're talking about.

Even the TV in the open door is a new
animal, the world news
abandoned over a month ago.

The cicadas I understand, little
jackhammer hearts, their business
universal as lightning.

The sun's white mortar trowelled
on my hand,

the eucalyptus, the pine-slurred
air,

sisters
I'd forgotten I had.

AT THE FOOT OF A WALL

My hand moves below
in the bright element, turning
a page. The deck chair's bleached

arms, my feet bare on the flagstones: all
mute, opaque as at home.

Nor are the cypress, the lemon, though trimmed with bookish
associations,
eager to break their poses and dance.

I thought sun and the island's beauties would dive
into my eyes, out of my mouth in poems.

Nearby, small lizards are skirting
the foot of the wall: quick
green marginalia,
foreign script.

Overhead, the Grand Prix. Burly helmeted flies come
whining down the blue straightaway over the mulberry tree
and smack the sun-covered house,

drop flat bullets around my feet. Tiny,
terrible headaches. Twiddling legs.

The lizards scribble, licking them up.

Green, independent flames.

PRIMITIVE RENAISSANCE

We travel south to a shore crackling
and aromatic, necklaced in salt,

then to an island,
white,
giddy in space, where shoes,
shirts, jeans wander off on their own and skin

remembers its language, bounds
into conversation with the world, skilled in a grammar it
never learned in the north,

sniffing,
yanking us off the path. Every object it meets
is its physical kin,

has a shapely ass
or anecdotes, invitations to meals.

At the sun-scarred table, heat
rustles the eucalyptus leaves overhead, pine
and oregano spirits brushing us.

My fingers find the cup's tiny
shape deep in its own white glare. Inspired,

we plan a high culture built
low to the ground,
a primitive renaissance.

Looking at you, I have never felt so wholly
at home in a country of pupils
and lips.

It comes around, if you let it.
The land comes around
inside the eyes.

Under the table, our starved feet are
pigging the cinnamon dust.

NOON

By noon, down to my shorts, I abandon
the upstairs table, my papers and books
in the slatted shade, the outside air
a white tambourine wildly
shaken, and tread the burning path
to the bathhouse,

dim grotto, shrine of the water tap, this
vein of the earth I open, sluicing
my face and chest – shearing a fleece
of heat –

             the dampened flagstone floor,
home of grateful scorpions and lizards;

then out again, squinting, jerseyed in clear beads,
I stand like a circus performer under the lion's
mouth

while the sun with its blinding
teeth (breath
smelling of blood)
picks each drop precisely off my skin

APRICOTS

for Ralph Bates

Sit down, sit, have some cucumber, some wine. I insist! Look,
that little chapel, you see it there on the opposite hill, is where
our *own* miracle took place. Not long ago. The year the ferry
began to come to the island. Some bread, bread and misythra,
eat, we make it ourselves. Young Despina here in the village,
Manoli and Evangelia's daughter, was blind from the time she
was born. She's married now, living in Athens, her husband's a
customs official, a man with family there in Galini. He met her
only a couple of years ago. She now has a child of her own, a
healthy girl, but she, young Despina, was blind from the time
she was born, or could see just enough to feel her way, tap-tap
her way like this on the trails where her father had goats. It was,
oh, how many years? The year of the ferry, the year of the apri-
cots. *The apricots!* The spring had been wet and then very hot,
and the trees were breaking with apricots all through the valley
here, and everywhere else. You couldn't get rid of them! In
Athens they offered *two drachmas a kilo*! Nobody would even
agree to *pick* them for that! And Despina was over there on the
hillside herding the goats for milking, and a voice, a man's voice
suddenly spoke to her: *open your eyes and you shall read the
book* – the Bible of course he meant – and she heard this, but
she didn't open her eyes. And the voice spoke again to her:
OPEN YOUR EYES, it said, AND YOU SHALL READ THE BOOK.
And she opened her eyes, and could see, truly, and came
running to tell us all. And in Austria somehow, in Vienna, they
heard of the apricots going to waste, and trucks came here on
the ferry, the new ferry, trucks with wheels as tall as a man and
machines to keep the fruit cold inside in its boxes, and they went
back all the way to Vienna filled to the top with apricots, and

paid twelve drachmas a kilo when Athens, those bastards, had offered us only *two*! And we built that chapel there on the spot where Despina heard the voice. You will see a painting in front that tells the story of this.

At the foot of Apano Kastro, in cold
wind, Ralph says his legs won't
work today,
comes to a stop, closing his eyes –
allowed only five nitroglycerine tablets a day,
and this is his third.

Seated on stones, we carefully show
no interest in whether his heart
returns to its perch or not.

The story he tells begins with what a shepherd
on Mount Fanari told him fifteen years ago –
how Ariadne, before she went to heaven, left
her crown in a cave near where they stood.
The shepherd offered to pay for a bottle of wine
if Ralph could guess what the crown was made of,
and Ralph said "parsley," and the shepherd
staggered back, wondering how Ralph knew,
and Ralph said it was in a book. "A *book*!"
the shepherd roared. It was his *grandfather*
told the secret to *him*! Offended,
he strode away.

Of course the man had
no money for wine, Ralph says as we get up
and walk again.

THINGS POURING OUT

                    blue
morning glories
        hang from the wall
    over the stairs and tables
playing a jazz of bees

I blur a bit
    fingertips on a beaded Heineken, cheek
    brushing houses built in the valley's
    far side, tender as lips
or nipples

talk, sun on the groups of faces, flows
    in the Sunday square   cool wafts from the open
    church doors, beeswax, dim
    stone

from a radio somewhere the voice of a politician
    leaks like a faint gas   laughter, noise of cicada
    traffic fill up the air   girls

in white ruffled dresses gravely pass
    in the back of a truck   the miniature
    politician menaces like a rampant goat engorged
    with himself

    amusing

but he'll have to die

SELF-PORTRAIT AS SAINT GEORGE

After burying the rat by the jasmine,
I notice glossy coils bulging between
stones at the wall's foot, their diamond
pattern in browns and greys – a sleeping
snake, near where my kids play –
and thinking of the two hatch-marked
adders I saw by the brook this morning
on a bed of old straw that drank them in
like laces pulled from below,
and remembering my neighbour's talk
of their venom, and the one I nearly
stepped on climbing Fanari – tantrum
of knots, its mouth the fizzing end
of a fuse – I know I have to steel myself
and roust this sleeping dragon out.

I change my sandals for rubber boots,
choose the tallest mop in the closet
and stride to do combat. Planted
Samurai style, I reach the handle out
to tap the shoulder of the monster's dream,
but the handle clanks on a hard coil,
a root? . . . ? I have no category
for this thing that should be soft.
I strike again, its skin shatters,
liquid spilling out – an egg? a snake-
imitation egg? – and at once I recognize
snails glued in a group embrace, and my
ghost
            hoisted over the treetops hangs

appalled at the freak in the garden –
skinny in boots, armed with a broom-closet lance
to do battle with snails.

VIVLOS

On the Volvo bus slowly
ramming its way through the lanes
of Vivlos, open windows slide
past like small subway stops, man
in a bathroom washing his ears, here
I could help myself to a breakfast,
flick on a TV, bras
and pillowcases tickling our roof,
a woman sticks her pregnant belly
out of a doorway, our shuddering
fender nearly touching her black
swollen skirt.

THE LANES

through Tsikalario,
climbing to dry fields,
houses in use and in ruin

run together, goats
in the roofless rooms,
wild figs. Voices

at one dark window
handling old belongings.
Hearth smoke, goat

smell: alleys into
the body, into the past.
Black dress on a fig

branch turns to me,
worn
briefly by the wind

GO, LITTLE LIZARDS!

Little insights that can penetrate
anything.

        Little birds,
the rocks are your air.

Your clean movements
remind me of smart people's faces.

I think I'd sooner be governed
by you.

BORROWED HOME

Alone in Jane's ancient house,
Alhambra of bookshelves and tea,
the cat curled on a chair, the walls
rubbed by the morning light tossed
in from the oleander leaves,
a shout jolts me out of the page
and the room's deep narrative –
a rough throat out in the windy
lane, heart's naked noise
flung at the closed doors, maybe
an idiot son of the fading Naxian
gentry, somebody's public shame;
I go to a window and wait for whatever
the alley is bringing, the slow
footsteps, the banished self,
the Minotaur's bottomless pain,
and there directly below, a gypsy
vendor is shouldering a hamper
of greens, lifting his rubbed-out
face, praising their virtues in words
like breaking bones, hoping to lure
the grandees down with his rural
goods, knowing their taste
for mountains distilled in food
and for rustic servitude,
the island's produce doffed
at their doors from sweating backs.
What is he saying? Oh come dear
ladies, look, fresh from the countryside,
sweet little herbs, delicious with
lemon, stewed with lamb,

they will brighten your eyes,
increase your progeny! But this
black-necked man in torn corduroys
passes on without a response.
He ought to be calling in English
or German or French, but he sticks
to the old Greek phrases that used
to work, unaware that the grandames
are dead, their places taken by strangers
in search of a past. I sit like one
of the listeners in de la Mare's poem
hearing him pass again, bellowing
for the old exchange. Only the cat
understands his words, her eyes
terrified, plunging around the room.

WIND

The poem makes itself
when it is ready and the poet
light-hearted enough in his grief
or good fortune

In the valley below Filloti
we had our lunch under an oak tree,
the wind blowing the paper on
which I cut bread

INTO THE NIGHT

Barefoot, the lamplit page
still in my thoughts,
at the millhouse corner I walk head-on into the
huge moon,

same stored smile riding
the childhood sky.

The olive trees, silvered and ruffed on the hillside,
breathe in the moon, fixed
in some night-long exchange beyond
what I can understand.

Grape leaves high on the trellis glow
slyly like clock-face numbers
gone back to the wild.

                    Owls' voices
pogo up at the moon all over the countryside.

Great goddess, since you are real,
art is the only work of any worth.

ANIMAL

THE GREEN INSECT

I had a green insect, a kind that had never before been
    seen,
descendant of an ancient nation, regal, rigid in ritual.

It would sun itself on my windowsill, stretching its legs
    one by one, its hinged joints, its swivel joints, its
    claws,
unfolding and folding its Swiss army knife implements.
It was ready for a landing on the moon.

Around my page it marched itself like a colour guard.
It halted, and its segments fell into place, jolting all
    down the line.

It uncased its wings, which glistened the way sometimes very
    old things glisten: tortoiseshell fans, black veils,
    lantern glass.

It was a plant with a will, an independent plant, an early
    invention wiser than what we've arrived at now.
It was a brain coiled in amulets for whom nature is all
    hieroglyphs.

People gawked, and a woman pointed a camera, and I
    hesitated, but – I did – I held the insect up by its
    long back legs like a badge, like my accomplishment,
and the air flashed, and the insect twisted and fought,
    breaking its legs in my fingertips, and hung

lunging, fettered with stems of grass,

and I laid it gently down on a clean page,
but it wanted no convalescence,
it ripped up reality, it flung away time and space,

I couldn't believe the strength it had,

it unwound its history, ran out its spring in kicks and
    rage, denied itself, denied me and my ownership,
    fizzed, shrank, took off in wave after wave of murder,
    and left nothing but this page faintly stained with
    green.

LEAVING DEER LAKE BY AIR

Our old dog gnawed his bone casually
and kept it around,
forgotten much of the time under the day-bed,
coated in fuzz.

This landscape, this old bone
gnawed in the same offhand way,
the woods roads like tooth marks,
the chewed and chain-sawed tracts of scruff.

This worn-out stub of a hairbrush
I live in
like a louse.

The time we were married, it was spring,
we were just into our twenties and a fierce
excitement was in the air, like the world was going to
reveal itself in some glorious way that summer
and only a fool or bloodless slave would have chosen
to stick with a city job – fluorescent shifts
in a sealed-window office block sort of thing –
and we got what they called a "drive-away" car
to take west, that was before the Japanese
import boom, and second-hand cars were worth more
in Alberta than in the east, so we picked up a V-8
Buick to drop off in Edmonton, just for the cost
of the gas, which was dirt cheap then too,
and we headed out for the prairies, which neither
of us had seen and the Rockies and the west
coast of Vancouver Island which is still a dream,
the Pacific rolling with life, the whole Orient
curling against the body of North America,
the luminous air, the distances you could see
that summer, but what sticks in my mind most
troublingly, like a glimpse of magic, the
epitome of the time, was that crossing the plains,
in our living-room suite on wheels, we kept
passing guys on motorbikes also heading
west on the straight flat stretches of empty road
who were just sitting there, perched
or reclining on their machines like fakirs
on flying carpets, not holding the handlebars,
not touching any controls. One guy was riding
side-saddle, his legs crossed, reading a book.
He grinned and waved as we rocketed past,

upholstery up to our ears.
Another was lying back on his bed-roll, hands
folded behind his neck, ankles on top of his
headlight, his shadow skimming below – fifty
miles an hour under the continent's sky,
ignoring the facts of physics.

The summer was rich in displays like that.

Where are you anti-gravity riders now?
You mockers of laws? Write to me care of
Grenfell College, Corner Brook. Tell me I'm
not making this up.

But you said . . .

                no.

No, but you said . . .

       didn't you mean . . .

no.

     But I thought . . .

and that photo you showed me of old rolled wire fence
standing up in the snow, metal maple leaves on the top
strand – apology
for being a fence –

              you had to open a drawer,
take out a box, take out a folder,
take out an envelope, take
out the pile of photos of where you grew up,
reach in,
        hand pushing liver and stomach aside
in the dark, your eyes' animal
vision –

very Canadian fence –

you called, you said . . .

               no,
no no no, but you said –

curve of your collarbone came to my front door,
soft skin over your collarbone, warm
nook
        where your neck takes
leave for Canterbury, mounting
a white horse tricked out in bells – a flutter I laid
two fingers on –

                hands, collarbone
racing around the house, out the window over the roof
and in again,
                yipping like hawks –

leaf-trimmed loosely rolled
fence, like a turn-of-the-century aviary

only snow inside

THERE IS NOTHING WAITING TO EMERGE

there only is
what is,

the snowy fields, unlike
any face,

the shift
at work at the mill,

Mars:
oceans of untouched dust
instead of the two-headed gurus we'd
hoped for.

This is a hard
pill
to swallow.

SAINT GEORGE

1

You might well ask – I used to ask
this – when the dragon dies
where does it go?

A mound of tentacles, fins, fading iridescent
scales lies stinking
while the scholars poke and sketch and try
to imagine what it looked like rampant.

Where has it gone?

I was the one who touched it
with my lance. The butt against my chest,
I felt the hard point judder and the shaft
slowly press its ribs apart.
Its whole will heaved in the wood between us,
but I bore down.

I had caught the rarest fish
in that vast ocean, pierced it
perfectly

and drained the ocean out.

2

When I had taken
the dragon's life

I felt rampaging
heat swelling
my body

I had to throw my armour
off
    before it burst

3

Holding my spear I walked in the moonlight
on a hill above Silne, its few lights
flickering, its dogs echoing on the plain –
a city dying of thirst,
with no reason to be where it was, its people
ugly, cruel.

On the white barrens, I seemed to be pacing
a frozen lake with some huge
creature swimming underneath.
    Then
at the start of a small valley, as my thoughts
were turning to dreams, I felt my wrist
turn with the spear's weight. At first
I fought with both hands, my spear
bending as if I'd caught a sturgeon
on a bamboo pole.

That great life and my spear
wanted to be together.

So I followed the spear, threw my strength
into its dive, which went half
its length into the hill. It happened
in my hands.

Then I sat, and sleep came up in waves,
and when I opened my eyes, the sun
sat on the plain's rim.
A hawk hovered.
I saw that my spear had pinned a large
snake through the back of the head.

From Silne they came to help build.
We placed the altar over the spear's
stump. In less than a year Sabina
was living within the walls, and up
the hillside wound a stream of people
hungry for her help.

4

perhaps there is a cavern under sleep
that can only be entered by drifting down
to the very bottom
forgetting all of yourself   not even
dreaming useful dreams

there you slide into the sleep below
sleep where your soul is free of your
boring company
at a party with its own kind
from which it eventually emerges with its face
glowing as though still thinking about funny
or beautiful things that were said
and it joins you again where you are waiting
and you follow along up toward
waking
hurrying to keep in step

a little flustered
a little in the dark and yet relieved
wondering what its purpose now
could be

5

after that my body parts
rained down all over Europe

my good arm thumping down on the altar
of Saint Pantaleon in Cologne
parts of my left arm scattering to Toulouse
and to the Abbey of Auchin and into the care
of the Countess Matilda
my head cropped up in Santo Georgio in Velabro in Rome
also in the church of Mares-Moutier in Picardy
and again in the church of Ferrara

What more monstrous thing
had I ever killed?

HOW DO I KNOW THIS?

When night has swallowed the Blomidon
Mountains, the people of Benoit's Cove
down on the coast, while they talk
on the phone or play cards in the kitchen,
are always vaguely thinking about
moose, high on the slopes above them,
loose as smoke, breaking
willow twigs with their morose
mouths, and this vague awareness of moose
is a musk of excitement around whatever
they're doing, like the promise
of sex – the nearness of those hot
shapes of blood, nameless dispersed
lives they can sometimes ambush and eat.

But at night the moose are not
where the people of Benoit's Cove
think they are. Unseen
in the dark, the moose are only the slight
sound of twigs crunching, only long
plumes of thought reading the smells
the wind carries from Humber Arm,
from the houses of Benoit's Cove,
and the moose travel the history of each
smell back to its beginning – fish, dogs,
woodstoves, deep-fried chips –
the moose flow down on these ribbons
into the homes of Benoit's Cove,
into the swallows of rum and Coke
which they smell very clearly,
into the cigarettes – wherever

the smells hover, the moose hover
very thick, an attentive cloud,
absorbed, fascinated, digesting
the molecule code, observing the way
so many smells enter and leave
the human body – the moose, pulled
long like very fine black scarves,
loop into and out of the people's
bodies as they think of their guns,
as they think of moose stew –

                             the moose
enter the bedrooms under the closed
doors, seep under the sheets and wreathe
the lovers in their own excited
smells –

        from high on the dark
wooded hills the moose waft
down in slow streams on the air
to wrap the bristling lovers
in peat-brown hair.

The camouflaged skink
of Newfoundland
is marked and fringed so much like the dead kelp
in which it shelters,
and mimics the kelp's smell so brilliantly
and moves so much like kelp flipped in the wind,
it is generally undetected even by fellow skinks.
It lives a long solitary life,
hunting small foodstuffs, and dies,
                              generally,
unmated, unmultiplied.
I crouch over the camouflaged skink,
my clasped hands trembling,
or over where I think it might be,
it is so like me, and yet
entirely alien.

The painted skink of Surinam,
which puffs its iridescent throat
in a shaft of sun and yodels in high
C and smells something like lamb tandoori,
can attract mates from miles away,
but more often ocelots, pythons, leaping
tarantulas.
In my palms I cradle the valiant
bones of the painted skink, the nearly
extinct painted skink, small

cogs from my own broken heart
I'll never be able to put back
together.

Christ! the lion *also* smells our pubic tufts, and we
uncouple and run like crazy across the savannah

ON A LAWN CHAIR AT NIGHT

I wonder who'd be fool enough to write
a poem about the moon,
chaste goddess, conductor of tides in great bodies
and small, on her spotlit podium,
prototype pregnant belly, prototype egg?

etc.

The smiles of a thousand haiku masters glide
down on her beams.

The black deep . . .

It *is* amazing having that big stone ball
floating around us up there,
our planet's planet,
a horsefly circling the head,
only not a horsefly, a miniature human being,
white, instead of flushed with our living hues,
a cold stillborn embryo,
a skull.

Oh the pale sick moon . . . too much of
her light and *your* skull will go sailing too, mooncalf,
lunatic, aaaaaaaaaa-ooooooooooooooooooooooooo!
She makes the sirens howl in the city,
she makes the hair stand up on the back of the neck,

even though nobody sees her there,
nobody thinks of her.

The hydraulic puppeteer still
pumps our various parts by our various fluids,
she's done it since before Stonehenge and the ancient Celtic
priests.

Our human faces formed watching the moon at night
the way we now watch the news,
with foreknowing and dread and satisfaction,
seeing ourselves up there, mythic,
shining with fame.

When I was fifteen years old
I would wade out into the night fields, the vetch and
chicory in silver billows,
and serenade the moon with a guitar: "Mooo-*ooooo*-ooon.
MOOOoooOOOoooOOOnnn," I would sing.
Don't ask me why.
It was the sort of sound I imagined the moon would conjure
out of the human mouth if she had her wish.
I was praying.
I wanted something badly.
A girlfriend, an interesting future, surprises,
travel. I'd known those fields since the chicory
was taller than me.

Once, on a full moon, with the crickets
white-hot, there was a hay-ride going by in the neighbour's
back field, and I climbed into a crab apple tree and
strummed and sang as the wagon
loaded with people went by beneath me.

They didn't hear me. They were singing
too loud themselves and looking the other way,
at the moon, or into one another's eyes,

or its reflection in one another's eyes,
and the guitar, one my father had made in *his* teens,
didn't have much volume any more.

It's right, there should be a kind of pale
heatless sun at night, making a short variable
entry, swinging her hip,
leaning against the polished piano.

Everything stops work and puts on special
clothes for the moon, like farmers
putting on suits for church,
worship still at the stage of courtship.
Trees do it best,
fluffing themselves with intelligent pride,
you can see waves of devotion like blushes rising, going
off them into the air in a white aura of disappearing
heat.

We should all have skylights over our beds so we sleep
in the moon, and those of us out of reach of a roof
ought to have moon-mirrors screwed to our windowsills,

we should all have one-storey houses with rounded
corners, and sit in front of our doors
in the moon's court,
learning again
the lost language of frogs.

This geology

still humming hit tunes
from a billion years ago, the same
hard rhythms taking you up to the rim of a
black hole.

Don't make me laugh,
people had never been thought of.

Whole lakes and canyons are what you can pocket and
take away.

You can use it, steal what your small
heart wants, it doesn't care, your dreams fixed on
manufactured toys. What does a skimming of trees count for
in a couple of million years?

Flit through and get lost, it says.

These mountains, these
long lakes
are still bidding goodbye to the glaciers.
And you?

ALBAN BERG

Seated, her long neck turned away
like a quarter moon in the low light, her
white arm stretched on the back of the leather
couch, her face, her shoulders beside the palm fronds
turned to the plate-glass wall, the sunset over
the city, effusion of fuchsia and tangerine
in the teal-blue west,

with Alban Berg weightless and intricate
in the dials' green glow,

in the floor lamp's mango pool
where she left her shoes.

The curved horizon, blocks and smoky boroughs,
the glinting avenues,
the traffic soundless ascending descending its twilit
scales, beads of light in long sliding necklaces,
the circulation of blood,
something fervent,
remote.

In the kitchenette, bowing, my fingers and knife
circle and court a lemon;
the glasses, the gin and ice flutter
under the close fluorescent light,

glossy
elusive shape. Yellow. The white rind
under the pebbled skin,

my fingers, ten white bystanders at the
scene of a –

the knife a curtain of chrome
and the nippled yellow character rigid with –

I glance through the door: across the carpet the
colour-soaked wall of glass, her profile,
her neck, touched with violet,
with apricot,
turns,
her face

sweeps my way in a
swath,

a white
road

God . . . interesting, keeping
bees in your kitchen . . . why
not, I guess, when you've got so
many flowers around . . . they
certainly make a warm sound,
I said *a warm sound* . . . well,
loud really, yes, I'd love some
tea. Where should I put my·
coat? I wouldn't want to smother
any, you're sure they never
sting even when they crawl
on your bare arms like that? *No,*
I'm not afraid . . . smoothly,
move smoothly, I understand, it
feels like 90 degrees in here . . .
and *busy* of course, I guess you
never feel lonely with this going on.
You do? How could you? And your
goldfish! I've never seen tanks
used as room dividers. Is it
okay to walk right in the pool
like that? No, I can see it's
shallow, but wait till I take
off my shoes and socks. An odd
place to have your table all
the same. How many kinds of
flowers have you *ah!*
I think I stepped on a fish,
no, *ah-ah-ah!* it was just
caught between my toes. Even
when they're in your hair

they don't sting? Just some
milk please. Lovely croissant.
And when the fish cluster
around our chairs like this?
Of course, they expect crumbs,
I know, I know, *smoothly*, but
how can you sit still with them
nibbling your feet? I keep
thinking it's jazz on your
stereo, *I said I keep thinking*
you've got some fabulous jazz
on your stereo . . . god,
I'm in love with you.

This time you're a man cutting fodder for oxen, alone in a narrow field overlooking the roofs of a village in Shansi province, your wife recently dead and your children down in the cities of Honan for years now, and just as you stoop, bundling the thick grass in your left arm, pulling the sickle blade close to the ground, you happen to notice far down the valley's road a figure approaching, his straight-backed manner of pedalling his bicycle, all right-angle joints, his blue cap and jacket, government issue through and through, some rare business bringing him out from the county office; and you watch, bending and cutting, your face brushing the sweet-smelling sheaves, as he nears the first village houses and children run to surround him, keeping a cautious distance, and adults too, out from their kitchens and sheds, and he shows some document from his pouch, and the crowd goes into a kind of contraction, a spasm, tightened and then flung out and growing, moving quickly, and it disappears, leading him, following him up through the village lane below you and you put down your sheaf and sickle now and wipe your hands and wait, with a strange closeness, a layer of intense air over your skin, because they must be coming up into the field near you.

It's your name they're calling, the first ones calling it still out of sight below the field's edge, and they're scrambling up now, pointing and running to gather around you in a ring, leaving a corridor for the brisk blue man of straight lines and angles who comes straight up to you in some kind of legend you seem to recall your mother or grandmother telling you, some kind of floating dream that's been waiting to happen to you for seventy-three years, and he opens his canvas satchel and takes out a folded paper and reads it aloud, then spreads it in front of your eyes, a wide plain covered in snow, the government seal like a fortress, the marching columns of words.

"Kuo Ping-chih is called upon to make immediate payment of $0.27 to the Ministry of Justice of the People's Republic of China for the purchase of one bullet to be used in the execution of Kuo Hsiang, his declared next of kin, sentenced to death for theft."

Yourself stripped and convicted. The shame in this far-searching visit from fate, a long finger down out of the clouds squashing a small cricket so recently chirping away in the grass. Your son! Young still in your imagination, taking food at the table, perched on your knee, though he was idle and devious later and fled in the middle of planting to Loyang to train as a millwright in the factories there and never came home. Sentenced to death for theft! Scrabbling always for more, impatient with this very field, this grass, the good it would slowly yield. And people more like trunks of forest trees to him, an unfeeling thicket to hack at and hide in, dark paths to run down, always alone. More like rooted trees in his angry mind, always, than many soft fingers of hands holding him up.

So the bullet, then, to put an end to what you began. The insulting small fee for the trouble of blowing him out. Not for the court costs, for his food in jail, for the pay of the soldier whose hand reaches out holding the gun behind his blindfolded head, but for the bullet only, smallest, cheapest, most common and mass-produced detail in the whole affair, most crucial and final implement, the naked directive breaking finally into the last innermost room of your son, where you should have intruded long ago to lay down the law, the space he refused to tidy and hang with official posters, where he never invited you, where he never played host, where he only wanted to store his trophies and gloat. You will hire the officer to break down the bone door to that room and sweep it out once and for all in a red wind.

The blue-sleeved hand shakes the paper once in a short command and you reach to accept it, your complicity in what will be done in a prison yard on the outskirts of some city near the sea, your punishment for not having stopped him, steered him more gently years ago in this field, in the village streets. You will be there, your finger not on the trigger, but inside the pistol's barrel. It is *your* fingertip the state seizes and uses to point at him, pokes into him, clicking him off. Your concentrated thoughts. Your property. The bullet comes out of you. The way you first shot him out of your barrel thirty-four years ago. All the good your unhallowed shooting ever did. Turn it to lead, they say, now, and shoot him again. The living skull of your son. They force you into the bullet's route like a passenger in a tiny train. His living head, bowed as he kneels, blindfolded, his hands bound at his back, his thick hair that you used to cut.

You will get the money, you say, and the corridor of your neighbours' bodies closes behind you like the trunks of a walking grove, following after down into the streets.

Twenty-seven cents. It lies in a jar on a shelf in the kitchen. Eggs that your hens laid that you sold some days ago. To go into this. Their feed and their clucking walk. Ridiculous tiny sum, with all the serious procession waiting to see it paid. The price of your son's life, all he is worth in the end, all your effort in making him was worth, your own essence, your own marrow revealed for what it is. And you pay the coins to blue girder-work man, the man like a blue seal on paper, and he places them in an envelope in his pouch and pedals away with your purchase, your thoughts, your marrow and seed and shame. To finish killing you far away.

my son, who's seventeen years old,
rides his bicycle to work in the heat and rain, and his legs and
    arms are bony and muscled

old men love to send them into the smoke
and trenches, into the knowledge of how easily bodies and
    courtesies come apart – we did it by jesus we did it, now
    you'll see

and for eight hours scrubs the burnt paint
off what he describes as iron grapefruit halves, assisting in the
    trickling together of parts from the continent's corners,
    some race of machines assembling itself in Karnac, Ohio, or
    Oshawa, my son labouring obscurely at the birth

handsome as never again, just getting his beard

comes home black with grease, proud and marvelling;
the other men, he says, don't talk about sports or politics, they
    talk about Ed's wife who's having her first baby, Ed says the
    baby's already dropped,

growing up in the country of my past, he'd often
had the shrines pointed out to him, the jobs from grade six on
    (35 cents an hour to start), heaving crates of rotten fruit,
    green bales of alfalfa, planks into the planer, planks into the
    planer

the rubber gloves they give him are like artificial
hands

working the wire brush, water spills
into his steel shoes, and the men who pass say *that* looks like
    fun

saving

lies in bed in the dark
smiling, sensing his growing invisible shape, his stories
    building

GRANARY

In those rainy villages the people
kept their grain dry in wooden
granaries on stilts, steep-roofed
cabins like sacred storks,
but rats could scoot straight up
the stilts and steal, and cloud
the whole year's meals with their
insulting stink; so the people
attached skirts of wood high
on each stilt – the barrel-makers
made these skirts of fine-grained
ash, waxed so no rats' claws
could get a grip on them – and,
on a patch of flagstones under
each granary, they put a house
for a dog, with an intelligent
terrier in front and a little
sign over the arched door bearing
his name – *Antony* or *Fidelio* –
and title: *Guardian of the Grain*,
so he'd be proud and diligent
in his war on the rats. To enter
the granaries, mostly the people used
oak ladders which they religiously
took down from the granary doors
and hung crossways on pegs fixed
in the stilts; sometimes they
worked out hinged sets of stairs
counterbalanced with a rock at the

top – with an easy tug on a strap,
even a child could tip these stairs
down and bring back a basket of grain.

What is it like to have your birth, your conception
    reversed,
shot back in a black shuddering into the stars to
    circle and wait,
moon's tiny twin,
orphan prowling the yard of the lighted house, the
    people behind its windows drinking, partying?

After six months and a change of government they bring
    him down into blinding light on a snow-covered
    plain, the TV camera waiting, under the blue,
inside the blue,
and he wriggles out and sits in the mouth of his hatch,
    crushed to the earth's vast breast, scarcely able
    to breathe,
his spirit soaring in bliss,
and crosses his forearms at his chest,

archaic smile.
The man has no body at all.

His oval eyes, his fine nose and lips are grouped in
    low relief on the white expanse of his face like
    Agamemnon's gold mask.

He shines in his silver suit like a popped seed.

From the low horizon, men in wool coats loom over him,
    lift him, sloshing side to side, to a lawn chair,
where they lay him as though to sunbathe in the minus-
    forty-degree air,

and pour their words over his features: we brought you
   down because you owe me two hundred thousand roubles,
   look he's thinking of his wife, his cock can stand up
   even if he can't, you left Doctor Piankoff's frogs'
   eggs in the station, we're sending you back up tomorrow
   to get them.

One spreads a shaggy robe over him.
One places a karakul hat over his cosmonaut's hood.
One hands him tea in a thermos cap, torch of steam in the
   hubbub of breath.

Hands mould the feeling of legs and arms and hoist him up,
   his head happily rolling,

to take his first step.

THAT NIGHT WE WERE RAVENOUS

Driving from Stephenville in the late October
dusk – the road swooping and disappearing ahead
like an owl, the hills no longer playing dead
the way they do in the daytime, but sticking their black
blurry arses up in the drizzle and shaking themselves,
heaving themselves up for another night of
leapfrog and Sumo ballet – some

trees detached themselves from the shaggy
shoulder and stepped in front of the car. I swerved

through a grove of legs startled by pavement, maybe a
hunchbacked horse with goitre, maybe a team of beavers
trying to operate stilts: it was the

landscape doing a moose, a cow
moose,
most improbable forest device. She danced
over the roof of our car in moccasins.

She had burst from the zoo of our dreams and was
there, like a yanked-out tooth the dentist
puts in your hand.

She flickered on and off.
She was strong as the Bible and as full of lives.
Her eyes were like Halley's Comet, like factory whistles,
like bargain hunters, like shy kids.

No man had touched her or given her movements geometry.

She surfaced in front of us like a coelacanth, like a face
in a dark lagoon. She made us feel blessed.

She made us talk like a cage of canaries.

She reminded us. She was the ocean wearing a fur suit.

She had never eaten from a dish.
She knew nothing of corners or doorways.

She was our deaths come briefly forward to say hello.

She was completely undressed.

She was more part of the forest than any tree.
She was made of trees. The beauty of her face was bred
in the kingdom of rocks.

I had seen her long ago in the Dunlop Observatory.

She leapt from peak to peak like events in a ballad.

She was as insubstantial as smoke.

She was a mother wearing a brown sweater opening her arms.

She was a drunk logger on Yonge Street.

She was the Prime Minister. She had granted us a tiny reserve.

She could remember a glacier where she was standing.

She was a plot of earth shaped like the island of
Newfoundland and able to fly, spring down in the middle of

cities scattering traffic, ride elevators, press pop-eyed
executives to the wall.

She was charged with the power of Churchill Falls.

She was a high-explosive bomb loaded with bones and meat.
She broke the sod in our heads like a plough parting the
earth's black lips.

She pulled our zippers down.

She was a spirit.

She was Newfoundland held in a dam. If we had touched her,
she would've burst through our windshield in a wall of blood.

That night we were ravenous. We talked, gulping, waving our
forks. We entered one another like animals entering woods.

That night we slept deeper than ever.

Our dreams bounded after her like excited hounds.